ER  MACHINE EDITIONS CHICAGO, IL   DENVER, CO

More Radiant Signal

More Radiant

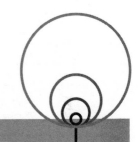

Signal

ACKNOWLEDGMENTS:

Some of these poems appeared, occasionally in different versions, in *Art New England, Aufgabe, Baffling Combustions, Conjunctions, Denver Quarterly, Glitter Pony, jubilat, Little Red Leaves, No: a Journal of the Arts, Skein, One Less, Web Conjunctions,* in the *Poets on Painters* exhibition catalog, and in the chapbook *Pie in the Sky* (Braincase Press).

Thank you to Noah Eli Gordon and Joshua Marie Wilkinson for believing in my work and wanting to see it in the world. Thank you to my teachers and friends, especially Peter Gizzi, Elizabeth Willis, Dara Wier, Natalie Lyalin, Sara Veglahn, and Sueyeun Juliette Lee. Much love and thanks to my family, my sisters, and also Michael, for everything.

Printed in Canada

Cataloging-in-Publication Data is on file at the Library of Congress.

ISBN-10: 0-9815-2274-2
ISBN-13: 978-0-9815-2274-6

Letter Machine Editions
P.O. BOX 608361
Chicago, IL 60660

lettermachine.org

Distributed to the trade by Small Press Distribution *(spdbooks.org)*

Cover Image: detail of "Jill Ann," Xylor Jane, 2005, ink on paper. Courtesy of CANADA NY, NY

for my parents

contents

More Radiant Signal

Habitat for Endangered Species

Thus begins a study of the secret life of the stick figure
whence the inland evolution of my imagination took place
Internal energy fluxes for example
manifest in both man-made
and natural lakes
or so says
The History of Lakes
I'm an alpha particle it says and you're
turning the lamp on
I'm radio luminescence
immanent architectural
I'm unflappable
I'm sure you're
unflappable too

Personal Drama

Camouflage in the katydid is better

I don't really know this from a cloud:

eyes at a pretty close distance
very good for walking

Whatever left hand you left in love

with Queensland, Australia
Lemon Grove, California

incomplete metamorphosis
almost clairvoyant

The Life of Marginal Fauna

No more a starling than a complex variable at odds with the limit and reach of her body. Not the inner majestic material medium nor the First International Polar Year. My location at sea and my fundamental empirical measurement of the earth a skirt of intellect in the almost blue darkness of Lorca. The speed of light is finite and cannot be altered. It enters the painting and remains there, advancing a wave in multiple directions of loss. To surmise the anonymous woman's untitled secret, open an aerial view of winter inside her. She must remain the bright double, the striking southern light in a painter's alphabet. The question is not "Will she dream?" but "Can she imagine a more beautiful bell or planet?" She is adjusting her dress and spectacles. She is adjusting her painting entitled *Interior Monologue Concerning the Use of a Single Color.*

Earth, Apple, Fly
after Barbara Guest

Was it reverie or commencement?

doing and undergoing

stars in the portrait

✦

"If my heart had been enticed"

the whole canopy of the heavens

had fallen   and fell

in her lap

4

Ambiguous Signature

Lush and handmade or lush and mechanical. The beauty is the icon never sleeps. At the end of an avenue a fine hammer, and a shape that revolts in a dancer also sees. My celery, my pistachio, my bug. Neither borrowed nor a figure. A living calendar, a spacecraft for sale.

Department of the Interior

Not between you and the birdbath, but the birdbath and the farmstand is triumphant. A happy confluence, says the dictionary. Between the Pacific Ocean and myself, something similarly transitive and dependent. Between the longitude and the conjunction of where I've been, we observe a given and a line passing through, from one side to another, from here to the moment before. This means I promise to join you at precisely half past the hour. I promise this meeting will be an encounter of great magnitude and proportion, expressed as "we," in the present perfect, "have encountered each other." Or, have you been smiling for a great duration, earth's equator, prime meridian?

A Red Bird

an adjective
a description
a figure or fugue
a continuous interweaving
of being or having been
an admiral
a red admiral butterfly
of the color red
of the long-wave extreme in the visible spectrum
and distinguished with
like an animal with a reddish coat
of having been left out
revised with red
wearing a red dress
or seeing red
seeing red sequoia
a love object
a noun a pomegranate
a flicker of red
a flicker
of light on the underside
of a wing

Confluence

A patient feeling I heard you say
a patient mouth absorbs the spark of a secret train

moving into the birdhouse to abandon the actual
our secret tender and electric paper boat

The point is to remove the self from the emerging
of the lucky and the disbelieving who are the same

A shiny noise makes a happy landing
insisting that life be the one tree, the one

happy signatory, form of starling

Hello calculator hello lucent opposite
of human

I didn't get lost when I went through
I gave away my salty velveteen when I divided

This was then and that was also

from inside this color bespoke
the paper bag over the theoretical head

of the living

My first syllable the wanted fox

of winter fall

In the end we will have the titanic the elevating and the harmonic
the rabbit quixotic as an imitation of a novel by Kafka

In this density of movable parts I can only love
the molecules I am about to become

when you are the maker of the fantastic
undressing a sunflower

implied sleeping iris

How lucky we are to have fingertips

how lucky the 1,000 verbs
will eat of the hand of their conductor

given the chance

Liminal workers in the underworld of the kind professor

the face of Aristotle also the conductor
of these colossal heads of sailors

I repeat

we are green whole zeros we are given the sleepiest glow
worm quietly falling

in this almost human of trains

This is Europa

We listen to signals, sinking in the margins of a final fig. If you come here in your navy, on your knees, and drink. These are the cells we smoke, the laws we ingest. We are census beacons or simple wings. If one of us whispered or left open the door. If we let our minds work all night in the dark. May it be a matchless lamp or a secret sign like stolen things, an involuntary gem or a green wave.

Several Always Before the One

Knee deep in what perspective
is a throat dark like a robin
and distinct from other seasons
in a fishbowl or factory
living on the last teaspoon of water
at the other end of winter
What thought did break
across these shins
what temperature
do I need to survive this
room despite all efforts
to hide myself beneath
the lacy undergrowth
of arms and legs like a button
pressed under the sign
of someone else's skirt

3:54 A.M. Pacific Daylight Time

I want astronomy I want you snowshoe

and evensong I want persimmon

Who is patchwork and also emerald

who is diamond

I want you raspberry I want whatever

I wear a swimsuit to the edge of town

I want you to see me

watery medium human being

planetarium

What I want in music is therefore Alaska

only different

I want you cinematographer

make me a picture

We are sleeping under the wool tonight

of California under the stars

I love

who assumes the shape of an elephant

who sounds like herself who hopes for the best

who laughs

in the middle of nowhere

a summer room where I shall picnic

If it's not too much

to touch the edge of something

who is lifelike

Pelagic

i.
You can make any kind of sentence illuminate the reader
a figure off-center is what I saw
any blue or off-blue rendition of childhood
an American backyard
That was a sentence and I am
a simple buckle to hold together
pieces of English
what the Latin surrounds

ii.
We're living in temperature
being in the manner of one
who is expanding another
expanding a text
I am reading
in mid-spring
in the neighborhood of twenty million
I should have mentioned before
We're not water birds
disintegrating on land
we're 6 feet tall
6 foot 1
5 foot 11 and a half
of another

iii.
I wanted to write these words:

plump indecisive shadow of parsnip

I wanted to save:

hummingbird flywheel four pocket

like the miserable folding themselves into liquid

who did likewise curse the alphabet

I wanted to know:

the housedress I am wearing tempers weather

little boats pretend

Quasi-Everywhere

From one subaqueous team to another. Piecework is a levy
that shall be fed. We who stand in the presence of bluffs and
curlers, who take our whims like tokens from the sidewalk.
A major leap over hydrangeas saves us, but tomorrow we are
partly sunny, almost old and windswept.

The Painter of Modern Life

Someone on the train announces
he tries to pile two lemons on top of one
he pulls paper over his mouth
plays a new game every hour
grapples with water whistles
notes in many tones
focuses here and there
on sunspots

I wish any number between one and eleven
any train arriving ahead of schedule
I wish to empty the boat
when the boat arrives
the vessels from the bells
I wish to receive
when the boat exhibits

A ride on a train is very exciting
My photo includes balloons
rifts and tears in the sky
Afterwards you are forced to walk slowly
and recollect your inner life
become a cow a moving pendulum
the sun

Friendly Composition

This is a phoebe bird without end, a sentence by Virginia Woolf,
the depth of the Mariana Trench. This corporeal, a pedestrian
inside of whom something essential. The insulating quality
of snow, a nectarine, this weathervane, these buttons. The
language we speak between blades of grass, under light bulbs,
waiting in doorways for friends to arrive, in the future perfect.
This shape we carry among our people, circle or otherwise,
when the sun is out, when the sun is an open situation. This
substance and design, this painting of a marigold. This will
make a real light, a found object. This epic version of yourself
on a winter night. This impromptu, this harmonious.

Encyclopedia

The cinematographer the elephant

a painter's vase illustrating
personal observations made during years of travel

The true cause of a solar eclipse explained
by a Greek who brings philosophy to Athens

now the famous paradox that motion is illusory

Tarkovsky's ghost in water

Pretext

What I want to understand
in the light that renders
the first human a real verbal animal
of hitherto unknown marine color
Elemental warbler
knocks my wind
A red verb to prehend and absorb
the management and flowering of flowers
that place in boxes what they see
of themselves regarding tomorrow
If selfsame can bend time
in a marigold to witness
the end of all water
Time must be an illusion
Much has been said
and much more placed
in an envelope

Amplitude

Define for me your imagination
the sevenfold speaking subject
eighth note falling
diplomat
who is you and who says
"This is me"
"This is my cherry tree"
Neither assassin
nor paintbrush bereft
of the dream
noise begets

No Single Binding Definition Has Been Found

I saw it
who would be made a motion picture of hills and comets

the edge of something
which is always hard to say

To dream inside the numbers five or six or seven

to think inside the dream
is a land to be lost in and to be from and not returning

I'm telling you something

a day is 24 hours

We're building a passionate lilac to give to the sun

how many other ways are there to say it?

On the Other Side and Far Away From Here

Flowerless dress, flowerless country
plus you, Nebraska
moving sideways through honey color

If one of us could follow
the maker of musical things
so the other might become
a real magnolia—
a composition of thoughtfulness,
of bioluminescence or whatever

No sound of plum falling
no imaginary friend

Illumination of the Earth for a Photo

In the future time will be construction paper orange
the heavens and all the spheres
will be construction paper orange
and the cat
walking between this world and the next
setting me on fire
with his construction paper color

Fourfold

greenly defiant pine trees
enabling each other
Eventually unscientific flowers
opening over the avenue
are the tallest buildings

intonation will follow
Mediterranean
and you follow or carry
chrysanthemums
singing or clowning around

Green's Function

Read the pictorial sunset moving backwards. Place the subject
in her boat. Address the hand as it leaves the body. Consider
the necessary element of surprise in the painting, the lack
of similitude before you temper the definition. Say goodbye
carnelian. Swallow the whole country if you can, the whole
egg about to unfold. Consider salt as currency and meanwhile
or further intuit the sun one letter at a time. Consider the
falling viceroy, his plum shirt, the quiet signature you make in
the sand, the glass, the inkwell, the mind alike in one mouth,
the humble boy, his leafcutters, the bottom falls out.

Therebetween

"whatever grace"
you are moving towards
the avenue facilitates

"the hollow of the ship"
the empty waist and eyelid
beautiful colossal
open *e*
You hold it

You light a match
You light a match and thus you create a flame

From the Interior of All Other Knowledge

Yes to circles that sound like words

Your posture measures the given possibility in a square

Real things are part of a body

Real things like oranges floating in the palm of a hand

Have you seen the green ray?

One possibility is to apprehend the immediate and material darkness

Another is to walk a little further

Questions for Trees

Does one arrive late to a station?
or does one
invite ambiguity into the mouth

Tulips invite hemispheres
imagining forms of survival

Something endlessly falls in the background
someone loses their hat, keys, mittens
someone arrives ahead of schedule

This brightness is no different from its absence
this photograph and aquamarine
Most secret friend
I will call you
a house or a finch in whom
I choose
one thimble
one hammer
one sound
two parachutes
or one shoe from one shoemaker

I dream of a certain color
a fascination with traffic
pulling apart the threads
of breakfast to find
the essential interior
farm
It's not enough just to oscillate
or be a monster
a knitted thing
a dual
hydrogen purple

The parallel or narrative revision of hibiscus
is holding the subject in place
Who sings this song, for example?
Who is doing the gardening?
Not the teacup
in your heart
Such luminosities need tone color
Human beings are never as big
as the water they carry

I don't know what you mean by that, but

The road is an image I meant to invoke
at noon, meaning infinite
"I am a humble swimmer"
I carry geraniums

and something else about nothing:
summer night
shining imperative

Who undertook to make this window?

who is on fire?

by the transitive property of
box elder beetle, pepper tree

the peach in my sentence:

distinction of a sunflower in the unknown quantity of Shakespeare

You can have relatedness I will take
January
in my side

The ambition you invent is wilderness in a walkingstick

and who you are

the author of this pine

I took you westernmost

I took you for a bicycle

I told you

"the mind must work upon"

the acre to build a body

from the shipwreck

Earth's own continuance at the limits

The Nature and the Material

I cannot say this animal is peppermint

citizen of abstraction or fisher cat

I cannot say the man in his house

his cups of twelve

I cannot say if he is

minus the fabric in his mouth

his middle *j* and silent *h*

his secret zero I place in cups

in all his secret zeros

A radical ambience remains

among trees

Distance times speed times

the triple bunting

the favorite fragment

of Euripides

I will tell you about his ghost

A median beginning in nine

dividing fellow from film

film from the blue outsider

Twice I embrace the handshake of the forest

twice permanent tilt begins

What takes place inside the dancer

in this arrangement of chairs and syllables

One will die grieving bereft of the other

while the other will remain

the peach-faced messenger the spider

totally sans bird sans letter

Impossible Object

The whole operation mumbles.
Some tiger lily swimming in the wind
picks up speed, enabled by
contradictions and moving towards
a more accurate description. Other
dimensions become home and we
float through public lungs. We've got
thinking to do or something else
like dividing a friendship in threes
and trumping the darkness, citizen.
Not even electricity yields religion and
surprise when the brain is a vessel
through which a little wind passes.
When you say I am a pirate and my
body is an image the mind makes,
I need this song in order to be
awkward. You can see from this point
of view, making a storm of public
disclosure, declaring, my head is in
Acapulco, my body in New York.
We're waiting for sunfish to interrupt.
We belong to the world by virtue of
grass. Look for the skinny, the surface
in the water, the character of vowels

when they open at the waist. Say you
once heard an operator speak softly to
a flower: "Forgive my grasp." You
declare yourself a longshoreman in
charge of a kingdom, marketing
problems to poets reading poems.
You must suffer less than I do from
superstition, regret. One might as well
paint pictures of books. In the room
of relevant misunderstanding,
you deliver the softest voice
in the middle: the cadence, the
hemisphere, the line. I lose patience
with the driver speaking English.
I maintain. I turn the page.

Paul Klee

How to compose a question: to spell the word blue
in Paul Klee's painting entitled *Paul Klee's The color blue*
in the painting the entryway to the little room called blue or
Holocene
a face with orange noise

In Paul Klee's painting *So many polar explorers*
So many buttons under hands
understand intimacy and texture
or substitute texture for
the intimacy under hands

I'm not your aster burnt marshmallow
small honey
gradations of warm honey blue to yellow light
pale suggestion of warmest chartreuse summery
suggestion of hello plus
Substituting the body for the
palest suggestion of green grass

Replace doubt with live color and the affirmation of color
or substitute affirmation with actual texture
substitute when a human body disappears
with wavelength or fold of blanket
substitute and/or replace wind
with bees

Fatal Bassoon Solo vs. *Well-Tended Woodland Path*
I knew myself to be on the verge of finding
the living record of an underground tree
I knew an ear was also an animal or
Witness the Man with the Beard of Bees
the cunning enticement of pen on paper

My moving furniture gave me
an uncompromising vision
like "signs intensifying themselves"
what is the shape of this meaning?
I've just cobbled together
I mean I've just jury-rigged
this hell hole
utopian ball

I'm thinking
of two syllables
a subject and predicate I stole
I'm thinking of
as knowledge relates to color, forms, the visible
I'm thinking
a grassy movement a texture
a diagram for the drawing of a line

Your birthday carries a wavelength and a color
your body carries this wavelength with specific reference to
"knowledge...the visible"

I was explaining my drawing of a curved line
I said, I didn't know, I said
in a system of circles and stars

I resemble the heart in that painting
the half face half-turned the red-headed painting
I resemble the pinks and grays I resemble,
he said, that looks like you and I turned
in the museum in the gorgeous room
that's not me I said that's you

Articulation

Someone is born in Bethlehem, Pennsylvania

Someone is a marriage of cells to a house

I think this is what it means:

To be speechless in front of a mirror

To hire geraniums

To be had as much as to have

Unknown Quantity

How many ways to exist?
I don't have a pencil
as if I could write this
I can't even think
You are the textual orange
between presence and absence
Wind in the subtext is my wind
Mom is in the alphabet
Simultaneously all of the gesture
you ever want:
mittens, war and calico

Two Ideas

Are you in love with a rutabaga?
I beg you
be a different   be a better
bluebell
People like to be inside
Cadmium green deep
robin's egg blue

        &

When history fits inside
a package of seeds
Floating open waterways
receive
fingers and toes
Here we are in America
learning to whistle

Two More Ideas in a Different Mode

The kite is a bird

today and it thinks

it dreams up

to its chest

in a flock of itself

        &

I am craving

salty paper to sink

my funny cheek

my salty window

at water's edge

Wintermint

collects noon in its shell
such that it is

To be self-righteous

to make electricity
in a bowl of cherries

After paper is mine

It sounds like
if sheep were a verb

I would sound like

Softer More Radiant Signal

Tell me more about
crayons, contingency
and winter fruit
polyamorous structural
locations we know aren't always the best
for human hands anyway
Tell me she is all worn out
from work
and thinking
the ghostly opposite
or optimistic messenger
a perpetual shoe shine
or softer
more brilliant
orange
I embrace
More palpable and more
Tell me we need
more rigor
more strings
more
disclosure
Tell me we need more
of what happens to bodies when bodies decide

to say what they want more of
More love in the vernacular
for example
More words like
longing, appetite, hunger
more bodies to willfully embrace
in summer kitchens
Tell me you want more sublimation
of history
by palpable whim
and fancy
More French in brunette
more four inside five
more singular features to render
clean of muscle, more
muscle
More of that feeling
that accompanies an unsettled
state of being
More of the condition of being
naturally disposed to several
different feelings
tell me more about these words
turbulent, euphoria, indiscrete

The Little Sound in the Middle of Simone

Sound of her in the *x* of you. Sound of *p* in paper human beings. Sound of salt in salty water and transitive verb swim, the sum total of wind and wind-bearing objects in the distance. A sound in Simone saying, shall I? Not the same as saying I shall or the sound of *sh* inside of Simone saying shall. Not sound of silent *e* in Simone or the sound of *e* in something unlike Simone. Sound of the windfall of *s* in wingspan or wisp of air. Sound of *l* in the middle distance of Gala apple. Unknowable things in the middle of Simone, in the style of Simone's voice and locution, in the size of Simone's tone and presentation. Sound of irregular Simone. In the hope of Simone if *s* is not an actual Simone saying yes, I am Simone. Sound of Simone unfolding in a secret language of color and texture. Sound of Simone in piano key for *p* next to *a* for the animal in her surface. Simone descending a staircase. Something to fall in love with: sound of *s* in Simone saying yes, the sound of *s* is something.

Aquarelle

Newest tangerine unfolds across the negative space I substitute
with the essential element of thumb inside walnut. If you've
come this far to trespass our collective braid of laughter. Say
hello to waxwing fingertips. Hello in a figment harboring
numbers. Say yes to the fallen baritone sailing onward into
the distant sound of intercontinental murmur.

Prairie Sonnet

In this country, girls are miles of low-fi accordions. A final
frontier: American renegade arts and crafts. Moving west and
southwest with the highwayman, they become a border of
mums. Even with a fork in the road and indeterminate weather.
Even if the road doesn't exist. Just the continuous rush of feet
in a hot country. Or a nonfiction account concerning what we
know to be the truth of love. Hum hum. Folk misanthrope.
Cupped sun.

Beginner's Mind

It begins the first
to take
and to take anything

In the middle of a boy
sun settles
Electric people

There is no end
to the shape of things
if your heart goes out

Why don't you watch the icefall
Why don't you carry a cardboard cutout
of what you believe

A Mechanical Substitute for Joy

What the sun reaches
doesn't equal the sun
This is a law
There are different kinds of folding
in a person's face
There is Laurel
who looks like Laura
and Simon
who is also Simone

＋

Before you were a passenger
folding butter knives
in your housedress
you were a membrane
like a rusty pocket
and private throat
a singular plum
an ordinary
singular dress

If what you're thinking
about aeroplanes
is what you know about writing
in the Pleistocene
Who disappears when the sun
slips behind a pencil
Who sleeps,
when pear substitutes
for paper

◆

So the boy is a train
if such a lucky submarine becomes
so perpetually haphazard a medium
and bereft of a shape
to engender
I should have said hello
I am a windowpane in love
with a bright whirligig
but so what

The Importance of Rising Motion and the Mechanisms Responsible for Lifting Air

If p equals all of my weight in wood. If n equals all of the life in traffic. If a watercolor of l is effortless science is subterfuge or biology. I erupts as facsimile. This creates an equation for fluency and a highway for sky ornament. L is for local or for laughter. L is for a lexicon of possible appearances. The visual form of how roads end.

Air and Space Museum

The composer of a symphony sends her signal into space. Her face is a hub for noise. A boundary for illness. Her eye is an assembly of human failure. Is a hub that assembles all modes of enunciation. All the variations assembled in sympathy with strings. All the stars a hub for sound. When the air was strong. The air was moving syntax. It was local air and it was local love. The boundary of the sky is a touchstone for enunciation. A mouth opens the word *ocean.*

Fullness and Form

My equivalent
My one plus two
My animal kingdom
take me anywhere
in the present tense
I am curious
Thus it was a pleasure to meet you
Thus in the mountains
I will find you

Lost at Sea

We live in the immediate neighborhood of our homes and
immediately again in a neighborhood of lamplight

and we embody an immediate texture of same and long for it daily
though we allow for a fine architecture to overwhelm us

or for a long-distance wave to find us. We've become animals again,
our senses tuned to the cumulous. We've honed our navigational

tendencies the way most ships and aeroplanes do regarding their needs
and rights for water and air. And regarding this situation of land

and rain, what's lovely in a thought is forcing an epiphany
or inventing a temporary iota of joy. We are fully blown

and operational, broadcasting at sea. Thank you for the report
of your transmission and for your clandestine operations.

Thank you for your tendencies they will be more than likely
in the event of a landing or in the hopes that we may fall.

Shooting Dreams

Summer shows muscle,
a handful of boy
in the parlance of bird
His secret method
is winter, but I believe
the peach is made of time
I believe my syllable
the glassy sweeper
a luminescent fish

Clouds are Temporary

By what definition is an element also
the double weight of pressure

by virtue of what is more
than a girl

A voluptuous Iphigenia among

my absolute sleepy curve
an intellect to fashion

and to myself reveal
an evergreen

✦

If in order to sleep
in the paragraph
of her own beginning

She who writes and comes to belong
to you

in order to climb

the Broadway and 78th
of her treeness

✦

To witness and partake
in something germane
to my own tree

My treeness invents itself
and is therefore germane
to the infinite plates and cups
of what is not germane
to trees and forthwith with other trees

and of the little apples
and of the fall

✦

I reckon
I live in my cannonball

and I in my snowfall
indiscreetly place myself

I with my telescope
and my telescopic night vision of night

am the one pine cone
the one who knows

on the bus among
the out of service magicians

✦

As if to release yourself
from an arboretum
you believe in

like a child in kindness

is the tidal yawn
of limbs

As if to believe a salty earthling
begetting salt
asleep in trousers

There is Manifest Among Us a Desire

If such a thought were in me
to provide movement at the level of writing

I would ride this train all over California
I would

and I would hum
I would sleep in both

White Polka Dots

Perseverance in the color light blue

I wore a dress

All morning gold and black

All morning warblers visit the tree

white polka dots meet

a new yellow

A piece breaks off and gets found again

by the whole

Medium

From a girl named
Margaret to an alpha
beauty   From a boy
named George to
the lunar rocket
Follow me into
a lazy susan   Follow me
and behold Orange,
Connecticut

Small's Paradise

i.
"I be my own person"

"I borrow this structure"

"I borrow your buttons"

"I name her Dandelion"

"I swim against the current"

"I fall away from the object
  into another object"

(minus Ariel)

  is a pressure inside Ariel

(to herself)

"The rabbit is not quite a symbol of the prairie"

  The rabbit is a pressure:

(minus thimble and sister)

The ecstasy of the lightbulb
can be attributed to Margaret

(Margaret):

"I believe to be electric in movement"

"I saw the spirit of the red lily
hovering above the red lily like a flame"

I died in a shipwreck

ii.
"Think of the whole page"

Let A give B an object *(z)* to give to C

Let big B equal little b

the hunter and the hunted

a caterpillar who delivered unto me

a spiritual impulse

Arrange the roses across the roses

A girl in a glass of water

is a real girl in a real glass of water

The optic illusion dahlia

rose and dahlia

balloon and water

arrange the glass of water

Palimpsest

Everything inside of everything else
fox and sparrow

crocus and plumage
you make hibiscus
who is also rose of Sharon

though you are nothing compared to chrysanthemum
who travels 5,000 miles and then some

"For you"
"I have never felt so alive"

Paper Airplane

Sleepy pigeons

weave shy fish

with Adirondack

three of seven

in sloppy trees

a telephone in milk

like a warplane

the kind with pants

and Emily

who is transitive

in Massachusetts

The Number One is in the Flower

Therefore in her arc is lily like
therefore

Her lights   Her hips at a tilt

As figure *l* she said
in parallel air
and shadow *m*

The total distance
versus the rings of Saturn

✦

We sing in real time before the fire
from a chapter in our book

with leaves in our throats at midnight
fluid vowel *a*

The number one is in the flower
coiled and unflown

In winter form   In movement

In perpetual revolt

JULIANA LESLIE WAS BORN IN Cooperstown, New York and currently lives in Santa Cruz, California. She holds degrees from the University of California, Santa Cruz; Mills College; and the University of Massachusetts, Amherst. This is her first book.

Letter Machine Editions

Spring 2009: Anselm Berrigan | Sara Veglahn

Early 2010: Sawako Nakayasu | Travis Nichols

Spring 2010: John Yau

Fall 2010: Juliana Leslie | Farid Matuk

Spring 2011: Peter Gizzi | Fred Moten

Fall 2011: Edmund Berrigan

Fall 2012: Aaron Kunin (with FENCE books)